Discovering
the
Caribbean

JAMAICA

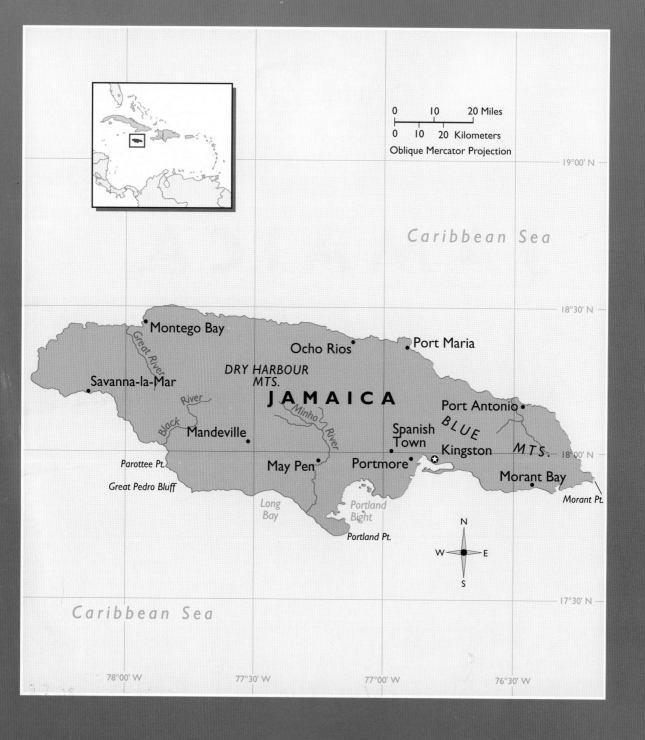

Caribbean Sea

0 10 20 Miles
0 10 20 Kilometers
Oblique Mercator Projection

19°00' N

Montego Bay

Ocho Rios

Port Maria

DRY HARBOUR
MTS.

JAMAICA

Savanna-la-Mar

Great River

River

Black

Minho River

Port Antonio

BLUE

Spanish
Town

MTS.

Mandeville

Kingston

18°00' N

Parottee Pt.

May Pen

Portmore

Great Pedro Bluff

Morant Bay

Long
Bay

Portland
Bight

Morant Pt.

Portland Pt.

N

W   E

S

17°30' N

Caribbean Sea

78°00' W   77°30' W   77°00' W   76°30' W

18°30' N

Discovering
the
Caribbean

JAMAICA

Colleen Madonna Flood Williams

Mason Crest Publishers
Philadelphia

Produced by OTTN Publishing, Stockton, N.J.

Mason Crest Publishers
370 Reed Road
Broomall, PA 19008
www.masoncrest.com

First printing

1 3 5 7 9 8 6 4 2

Library of Congress Cataloging-in-Publication Data

Williams, Colleen Madonna Flood.
Jamaica / Colleen Madonna Flood Williams.
        p. cm. — (Discovering the Caribbean)
Summary: Discusses the land, the history, the economy, the people, and the festivals of
Jamaica.
Includes bibliographical references and index.
ISBN 1-59084-294-4
1. Jamaica—Juvenile literature. [1. Jamaica.] I. Title. II. Series.

F1868.2 .W57 2003
972.92—dc21

2002070114

Discovering
the
Caribbean

Bahamas		**Jamaica**
Barbados	**Caribbean Islands:**	**Leeward Islands**
Cuba	**Facts & Figures**	**Puerto Rico**
Dominican Republic		**Trinidad & Tobago**
Haiti		**Windward Islands**

Table of Contents

Discovering the Caribbean

James D. Henderson

THE CARIBBEAN REGION is a lovely, ethnically diverse part of tropical America. It is at once a sea, rivaling the Mediterranean in size; and it is islands, dozens of them, stretching along the sea's northern and eastern edges. Waters of the Caribbean Sea bathe the eastern shores of Central America's seven nations, as well as those of the South American countries Colombia, Venezuela, and Guyana. The Caribbean islands rise, like a string of pearls, from its warm azure waters. Their sandy beaches, swaying palm trees, and balmy weather give them the aspect of tropical paradises, intoxicating places where time seems to stop.

But it is the people of the Caribbean region who make it a unique place. In their ethnic diversity they reflect their homeland's character as a crossroads of the world for more than five centuries. Africa's imprint is most visible in peoples of the Caribbean, but so too is that of Europe. South and East Asian strains enrich the Caribbean ethnic mosaic as well. Some islanders reveal traces of the region's first inhabitants, the Carib and Taino Indians, who flourished there when Columbus appeared among them in 1492.

Though its sparkling waters and inviting beaches beckon tourists from around the globe, the Caribbean islands provide a significant portion of the world's sugar, bananas, coffee, cacao, and natural fibers. They are strategically important also, for they guard the Panama Canal's eastern approaches.

The Caribbean possesses a cultural diversity rivaling the ethnic kaleidoscope that is its human population. Though its dominant culture is Latin American, defined by languages and customs bequeathed it by Spain and France, significant parts of the Caribbean bear the cultural imprint of

A Rastafarian man looks out a window in Ocho Rios.

Northwestern Europe: Denmark, the Netherlands, and most significantly, Britain.

So welcome to the Caribbean! These lavishly illustrated books survey the human and physical geography of the Caribbean, along with its economic and historical development. Geared to the needs of students and teachers, each of the eleven volumes in the series contains a glossary of terms, a chronology, and ideas for class reports. And each volume contains a recipe section featuring tasty, easy-to-prepare dishes popular in the countries dealt with. Each volume is indexed, and contains a bibliography featuring web sources for further information.

Whether old or young, readers of the eleven-volume series DISCOVERING THE CARIBBEAN will come away with a new appreciation of this tropical sea, its jewel-like islands, and its fascinating and friendly people!

(Opposite) Tourists visit Dunns River Falls, a popular attraction near Ocho Rios. (Right) A rainbow arcs across the Blue Mountains, which run through Jamaica and include the island's highest peak.

1 Jamaica's Jammin' Geography

JAMAICA'S GEOGRAPHY IS truly "jammin'," a Jamaican term that means "fun" or "enjoyable." This tropical jewel is a wild combination of beaches, grassy plains, mountains, valleys, jungles, *cays*, and raised areas of *limestone* and rock. Tourists and travelers from all corners of the world have admired the wild beauty of Jamaica's land and sea for hundreds of years.

Jamaica, the largest English-speaking country in the Caribbean, occupies the third-largest island in the *Greater Antilles*. The island is about 146 miles (235 kilometers) long and ranges in width from approximately 22 to 55 miles (35 to 89 km). Over half of the island nation of Jamaica sits at elevations greater than 1,000 feet (305 meters) above sea level. Jamaica's jagged coastline is 635 miles (1,022 km) long. Kingston, St. Ann's Bay, and Montego Bay are a few of Jamaica's better-known harbors.

9

The Interior Uplands

Most of Jamaica's interior is mountainous terrain. These "inland uplands" begin their rise in the western half of the island. They run through the middle of the island, growing taller and taller as they extend eastward. The tallest mountain peak in Jamaica, Blue Mountain Peak, is in the east. It is part of the Blue Mountain range. Standing 7,401 feet (2,256 meters) tall, Blue Mountain Peak overlooks the entire island. On a clear day at the top of Blue Mountain Peak, visitors can see the island of Cuba, which is almost 100 miles (160 km) to the north.

To the west of the Blue Mountains are the Port Royal Mountains. The highest peak in the Port Royals is St. Catherine's Peak. It stands a majestic 5,069 feet (1,546 meters) tall.

Along the eastern edge of the country, in Portland *Parish*, are the John Crow Mountains. These mountains rise to a height of approximately 3,700 feet (1,129 meters) above sea level. The John Crow Mountains tower above the shorelines of eastern Portland and then drop down to meet the shores of the Caribbean Sea.

The Limestone Plateau

Approximately two-thirds of the island of Jamaica is covered by areas of limestone and rock. These harsh-looking *plateaus* and ragged rocky regions are scattered between mountains and plains across the entire face of the island. One of the most interesting and best-known limestone regions is the Cockpit Country. It is in the interior of the western half of the island.

Much of the Cockpit Country is uninhabited. The terrain here is covered with deep pits and dangerous crevices. Travel throughout much of the region is limited to foot traffic, as cars cannot cross the rocky landscape.

The Cockpit Country is also home to Jamaica's Windsor Caves. The Windsor Caves are the birthplace of the Martha Brae River, which rushes along loudly deep inside the caves, particularly during the rainy season.

Rivers and Springs

Many of Jamaica's rivers originate in the country's mountains and hills. This makes most of them very difficult to sail down, or navigate, because they are prone to waterfalls. The Rio Grande, Martha Brae, and White are

Stalactites in Windsor Caves. This fascinating spot is located in the western half of the island.

Quick Facts: The Geography of Jamaica

Location: island in the Caribbean Sea, south of Cuba

Area: (slightly smaller than Connecticut)
  total: 4,243 square miles (10,990 sq km)
  land: 4,181 square miles (10,830 sq km)
  water: 62 square miles (160 sq km)

Climate: tropical; hot, humid; temperate interior

Terrain: mostly mountains, with narrow, discontinuous coastal plain

Elevation extremes:
  lowest point: Caribbean Sea—0 feet
  highest point: Blue Mountain Peak— 7,401 feet (2,256 meters)

Natural hazards: hurricanes (especially July to November)

Source: CIA World Factbook 2002.

among the few rivers that run along level ground.

The longest of Jamaica's 120 rivers is the Black River, which flows for 44 miles (71 km) from northern Manchester Parish through the Cockpit Country and the parish of St. Elizabeth. It finally empties into Black River Bay.

Besides rivers, Jamaica has many thermal springs. One of the more unusual springs is located in Bath, Jamaica. The spring at Bath is unusual because it produces both hot and cold water. The hot water reaches temperatures as high as 128°F (53°C). The mineral waters of Bath Spring are said to have healing powers and were once frequently visited by colonial English noblemen and their wives.

Climate

Jamaica's lowlands experience tropical climate conditions cooled by the northeastern trade winds. The lowlands of Jamaica boast an average daily temperature of 80°F (27°C). The average daily temperature in the plateau and mountainous regions of Jamaica is 72°F (22°C).

May through June and September through October are Jamaica's wettest months. While these are the rainy seasons for the entire island, Jamaica's average rainfall varies widely from region to region. Kingston receives about 32 inches (81 cm) of rain per year. Jamaica's northeastern mountains receive over 200 inches (500 cm) of rain per year. The country's annual rainfall averages about 78 inches (198 cm).

The official hurricane season in Jamaica is

Rio Grande rafters near the end of their voyage, just west of Port Antonio. The Rio Grande is one of the few Jamaican rivers that can be navigated easily.

from June 1 to November 30. Most hurricanes that have hit the island have occurred before the end of September, however. Hurricane Gilbert, which struck the island in September 1988, is still remembered for its severity. This hurricane left about 500,000 Jamaicans homeless. The monstrous winds from

A Jamaican man cleans up in the aftermath of Hurricane Gilbert. In September 1988 the hurricane devastated the island, leaving 500,000 people homeless and destroying an estimated $50 million in banana, coffee, sugarcane, and other crops.

the hurricane ripped the roofs off an estimated 80 percent of the island's homes. Forty-five Jamaicans were killed during this natural disaster.

Jamaicans have a traditional rhyme that reminds them of which months to beware of hurricanes:

June too soon, July stand by,

August prepare you must,

September remember,

October all over.

Flora and Fauna

Jamaica is truly a tropical garden. An astounding variety of orchids—237 different types—grow in this island paradise. Air plants, ferns, gingers, impatiens, and pineapples also thrive. Among Jamaica's trees are cedar, mahogany, rosewood, coconut palm, and allspice, along with logwood, ebony, palmetto palm, and mahoe.

Jamaica is also a paradise for bird-watchers. Over 200 species of birds are native to the island. Bird-watchers travel to Jamaica to view yellow-billed and black-billed parrots, arrow-headed warblers, Caribbean doves, becards, yellow-shouldered grassquits, and many other species.

Very few native mammals are found on the island of Jamaica. There are some wild hogs, goats, a variety of bats, and the endangered Jamaican hutia, a small, reddish-brown rodent similar to a guinea pig. Cows, horses, and other domesticated mammals were all brought to the island by settlers.

(Opposite) This detail from a colorful mural shows Jamaicans harvesting sugarcane, a staple crop of Jamaica's colonial period. (Right) British and Jamaican officials clasp hands in a gesture of solidarity after the final session of the Jamaica Independence Conference, 1962. The man on the right is Norman Manley, who would become Jamaica's first president.

2 "Land of Wood and Water"

SOMETIME AROUND THE year A.D. 700, Arawak Indians from South America settled in Jamaica, calling it Xaymaca, or the "land of wood and water." The Arawaks hunted, fished, planted, and gathered food from the fertile soils and seas of Xaymaca. They traded with the American Indians of neighboring islands, becoming well known for their spinning and weaving as well as their boat-building skills. They prospered on the beautiful island and established over 200 different settlements.

On May 5, 1494, Christopher Columbus first arrived in Xaymaca. His ship landed in what is now known as St. Ann's Bay, which he called Bahía Santa Gloria. For almost 150 years following the arrival of Columbus, Xaymaca was called Santiago. It served as a Spanish way station for ships sailing to and from the northern coast of South America, also called the Spanish Main.

Jamaica became a Spanish colony in 1509. Spanish settlers soon began farming the island for sugar and cacao, the beans used to make chocolate. The Arawak people were enslaved and forced to work in the fields. They soon died out, struck down by European diseases and harsh treatment. To replace them, the Spanish began shipping slaves to Jamaica from West Africa.

Jamaica was taken from the Spanish in 1655 by an English naval fleet under the command of Sir William Penn. (Penn's son would found the English colony of Pennsylvania in the 1680s.) In 1670 Spain and England signed the Treaty of Madrid. This treaty made Jamaica the official property of England.

A Slave-based Economy

Toward the end of the 17th century, more and more English immigrants came to Jamaica. They expanded the sugar and cacao plantations, creating an increasing demand for slave labor. Jamaica quickly became one of the biggest slave markets in the world.

In 1830 *mulattos*—people of mixed white and black ancestry—were *enfranchised*. The English government granted them full rights as English citizens. Blacks, however, retained their lowly status as slaves.

One educated slave, "Daddy" Sam Sharpe, came up with a plan to end slavery. He called for slaves to demonstrate peacefully against slavery by refusing to work for a day. Unfortunately, the slaves' anger had reached a boiling point. Violence erupted on Christmas Day in 1831. The slaves burned estates and killed a few plantation owners. To put down this "Christmas Rebellion," the colonial government imposed *martial law* and sent soldiers to fight the slaves.

After the rebellious slaves surrendered their weapons, they were punished. Over 400 slaves were hanged. Many more were whipped and beaten. The governor had promised all slaves who surrendered a full pardon, but he did not keep his word. Sam Sharpe was thrown into prison and then executed in 1832.

News of this massacre reached England, and soon the English were pressuring their government to abolish slavery. Thanks to this pressure, on August 1, 1838, slavery was abolished in Jamaica. By 1840, many blacks and mixed-race Jamaicans had gained the right to vote.

Plantation owners were compensated for freeing their slaves. The total sum paid out to slave owners was between $20 million and $30 million. The slaves received only their freedom.

Post-Slavery Woes

The end of slavery was a disaster for Jamaica's plantation owners. Unaccustomed to paying for

Christopher Columbus landed on Jamaica in 1494, during his second voyage to the New World. On his fourth voyage, in 1504, he stayed on Jamaica for an extended period in order to repair his ships. Five years later the first Spanish colony was established on Jamaica; the island remained a Spanish colonial possession until 1655, when it was captured by the English.

labor, they offered very low wages to their former slaves. Most of these offers of employment for starvation wages were turned down by freed slaves. They were determined to make it on their own. Many moved into the island's unpopulated interior. The plantation economy began to falter.

To solve the labor shortage, the government brought *indentured servants* from India and China. Workers came from Scotland, Ireland, and Germany. Free Africans traveled across the seas to Jamaica's balmy beaches. To the dismay of many of the plantation owners, few of these new laborers chose to work for their poor wages. Instead, they sought out small plots of land to farm themselves.

The Jamaican sugar plantations were now faced with increased labor costs and competition from Brazilian and Cuban sugarcane and cheap European sugar beets. Many failed, and owners abandoned their plantation manor houses. Large plantation fields, once used to grow acres and acres of sugarcane, became overgrown by natural vegetation.

The American Civil War added to Jamaica's economic problems. Already unsettled by the *abolition* of slavery, Jamaica's economy floundered as naval blockades cut off trade with the United States.

The population became unruly as a result of high food prices, inequality in legal practices, and the continuing decline of the economy. In 1865 a group of demonstrators marched to the courthouse in Morant Bay. They were led by Paul Bogle, a black Baptist deacon. Local soldiers fired into the crowd, killing dozens of protestors. The protestors fought back, burning down the courthouse and killing some soldiers. Governor Edward Eyre sent troops to stop the Morant Bay Rebellion. Over 400 rebels were killed and many others were whipped or beaten. In addition, thousands of homes were burned to the ground. Bogle and many of his followers were captured and hanged.

The governor blamed the uprising on a political opponent, mulatto assemblyman George William Gordon. Gordon was a friend of Bogle's and often spoke out against the government. Gordon was arrested, tried, and hanged.

The Rise of Tourism and the Banana Trade

Once again, the outcry in England was particularly loud. Governor Eyre was removed from office. The English Parliament took control of the government of the troubled colony. The English quickly began to build up the island's failing economy. They created a public education system and a civil service system. They also moved the nation's capital from Spanish Town to Kingston.

England also earmarked money for the creation of an effective road system in Jamaica. The Land Department was established to help sell government lands to farmers. The department filled marshes to create more usable lands. And in 1869 the English installed a telegraph system to meet the island's growing need for improved communications.

Around the year 1866, Captain Lorenzo Dow Baker began transporting bananas from Montego Bay to Boston, Massachusetts. Americans liked the unfamiliar tropical fruit. Baker soon established a successful business called the Boston Fruit Company. His banana ships began taking passengers on their voyages to and from Jamaica. With the rise of tourism and the banana trade, Jamaica's economy began to improve.

Unfortunately, in the early 1900s Jamaica was struck by a series of natural disasters. An earthquake killed over 800 people in Kingston on January 14, 1907. Hurricanes pummeled the island's shores in 1915, 1916, and 1917.

Labor Unrest

At the end of the 1920s, a different kind of disaster struck. On October 29, 1929, the American stock market crashed. This marked the beginning of the Great Depression. This massive economic slowdown soon spread throughout the world. Jamaica was not left out. Banana and sugar sales plunged.

Throughout the 1930s, conditions for the working class continued to worsen. More than 75 percent of Jamaica's population was unemployed. People were protesting and rioting in the streets. The economic and social gulf between whites, mulattos, and blacks had grown too wide. Jamaica's blacks were ready to fight for political power.

This new black pride was inspired by the teachings of the black leader Marcus Garvey. Garvey founded the Universal Negro Improvement Association (UNIA) and fought to gain equality and better working conditions for Jamaica's blacks. He encouraged blacks to think of themselves as a strong, united people.

In 1938 a large demonstration occurred at the West Indies Sugar Company factory. Unemployed workers seeking jobs at the factory faced off with police. A battle between the two groups ensued, and several people were killed in the violence. Jamaica became a violent battleground of looters, protestors, and strikers.

After the riots, two men emerged as leaders on the Jamaican political front. One was Alexander Bustamante, the son of an Irish father and a mixed-race mother. The other was Norman Washington Manley, who was Bustamante's friend, cousin, and ally.

Bustamante formed the Bustamante Industrial Trade Union (BITU). Manley formed a group called the People's National Party (PNP). Initially, the PNP was a subdivision of the BITU. But as the years passed, Bustamante and Manley began to have differences of opinion. The two groups split. The BITU then changed from a labor union to a political party, calling itself the Jamaica Labour Party (JLP). Bustamante was, of course, head of the JLP.

In 1944, England gave Jamaica a new constitution that provided for an elected legislature. It also called for *universal suffrage*. The JLP and PNP faced off to see who would win control of the House of Representatives.

Jamaican-born Marcus Garvey (1887—1940) was a promoter of "black nationalism." This was a movement to establish an African nation that would be free of European colonialism. After moving to the United States, in 1914 Garvey organized the Universal Negro Improvement Association (UNIA) and the African Communities League. Though Garvey's ideas were initially received with enthusiasm, his plans soon faltered, and by the mid-1920s he was in prison for fraud. Garvey eventually returned to Jamaica, where he tried to become involved in politics, but he was defeated at the polls.

Bustamante's JLP won more than 41 percent of the vote. Still, in 1949, when England allowed Jamaica to elect its own prime minister, Norman Manley was the people's choice.

An Independent Jamaica

On August 6, 1962, Jamaica became an independent state. Elections were held shortly thereafter. Bustamante was victorious this time and became the first prime minister of independent Jamaica. In 1967 Bustamante retired. He was succeeded by Hugh Lawson Shearer. In 1968 Jamaica helped to found the Caribbean Free Trade Area (CARIFTA).

Throughout the early 1970s, Jamaica's economy improved steadily. There was a great demand for Jamaica's supply of *bauxite*, which is used to manufacture aluminum. Unfortunately, the working class remained poor as the rich grew richer.

In 1972, PNP politician Michael Manley, son of Norman Manley, came into power. Manley promised to improve the economy, but failed to do so. He had ties to Cuban leader Fidel Castro, who was a *Communist*. Manley's *socialist* policies further divided the nation.

While Manley was in office, middle-class Chinese-Jamaicans began leaving the country in great numbers. Upper-class Jamaicans of all cultural backgrounds also began moving to the United States and Canada. Violence

Percival James Patterson was reelected to a second term as Jamaica's prime minister in 2002.

erupted throughout the nation, and as a result, tourism began to decline. Jamaica was floundering once again.

In 1980 a violent election campaign rocked the nation. Michael Manley was running for reelection against Edward Seaga of the JLP. Almost 800 Jamaicans were killed during the fighting between political gangs. Finally, after bloodshed that brought Jamaica to the brink of a civil war, Jamaicans voted Seaga into office.

Seaga was a former finance minister. He immediately took steps to improve Jamaica's economy. He distanced Jamaica from Fidel Castro and sought closer ties with the United States. Seaga also tried to improve the Jamaican economy by attracting foreign investors.

In 1988, Hurricane Gilbert demolished much of the island. Mineral export prices dropped. Despite Seaga's best efforts, the economy was not improving. The Jamaican people responded by granting the PNP a large parliamentary majority in 1989. Michael Manley returned to the office of prime minister, only to resign because of health issues in 1992.

P. J. Patterson succeeded Manley as prime minister and was elected to the office in 1993. In 1997, the PNP won its third consecutive electoral victory. The party took 56 percent of the vote and won the majority of the seats in Jamaica's Parliament. In 2002, Prime Minister Patterson won reelection and his party retained its majority in Parliament. The campaign and election were mostly free of the violence that had marred previous elections.

(Opposite) Small, colorful sailboats wait for tourists on a beach near Discovery Bay. (Right) A power shovel loads bauxite onto a dump truck. Bauxite is a key part of aluminum production, and Jamaica is one of the world's largest providers of this mineral.

3 A Fluctuating Economy

JAMAICA'S ECONOMY DEPENDS to a large extent on finding markets for its exports. This has caused Jamaica's economy to be somewhat unstable. As worldwide demand for sugar, bananas, *alumina*, bauxite, and rum rises and declines, Jamaica's economy fluctuates.

Jamaica has a wide trade imbalance—it imports some $3.1 billion worth of goods a year, or nearly twice as much as it exports ($1.6 billion). The United States is the largest market for Jamaican goods, followed by the countries of the European Union, the United Kingdom, Canada, and Jamaica's Caribbean neighbors.

Since the early 1990s tourism has slowly increased as Jamaica's government has aggressively promoted the island to foreign tourists.

Industrial and Service Sectors

The mining industry in Jamaica is driven by the world's need for bauxite, or "red gold." Bauxite is used in the production of aluminum. Jamaica is the world's third-largest bauxite and processed-alumina producer.

Workers sort coffee beans at the Mavis Bank central factory. Coffee beans, which are grown in the Blue Mountains, are among Jamaica's most important agricultural products.

Other industries include textile manufacturing, food processing, distillation of rum (a type of alcohol), and manufacturing of cement, metal, paper, and chemical products.

Tourism is an important part of Jamaica's economy. Approximately 40 to 50 percent of Jamaica's foreign income comes from tourists. More than 70,000 Jamaicans work directly in jobs created by the tourism industry. It is estimated that at least another 215,000 Jamaicans work in jobs that are indirectly related to the tourism industry. In 2001 visitors to Jamaica spent an estimated $2.5 billion.

Jamaica's Ministry of Tourism has fought to eradicate crimes against tourists, to educate Jamaican students on the benefits of the tourist industry for Jamaica, and to build up environmental tourism, tourist attractions, and resorts.

The film industry has begun to use Jamaica

Quick Facts: The Economy of Jamaica

Gross domestic product (GDP*):
$7.784 billion
GDP per capita: $2,720
Inflation: 6.9%
Natural resources: bauxite, gypsum, limestone
Agriculture (7% of GDP): sugarcane, bananas, coffee, citrus, potatoes, vegetables; poultry, goats, milk (2000 est.)
Services (60% of GDP): tourism, government services (2000 est.)
Industry (28% of GDP): bauxite, textiles, food processing, light manufactures, rum, cement, metal, paper, chemical products (2000 est.)

Foreign trade:
Exports—$1.6 billion: alumina, bauxite, sugar, bananas, rum
Imports—$3.1 billion: machinery and transport equipment, construction materials, fuel, food, chemicals, and fertilizers
Exchange rate: $49.5 Jamaican = U.S. $1 (October 2002)

*GDP = total value of goods and services produced in a year.
Figures are 2001 estimates unless otherwise indicated.
Sources: World Bank; CIA World Factbook 2002.

more and more frequently. It is a perfect setting for beautiful tropical island and beach scenes. Since the 1960s, motion pictures filmed in Jamaica include the James Bond movie *Live and Let Die*, Tom Cruise's *Cocktail*, and Robin Williams's *Club Paradise*. In addition, scenes for TV shows, such as the soap opera *As the World Turns*, have also been shot in Jamaica.

Agricultural Sector

Farming employs about 21 percent of Jamaicans, although it contributes just 7 percent of the country's ***gross domestic product*** (a measure of the total value of goods and services produced in a year). The most important crops include sugarcane, bananas, coffee, citrus fruits, potatoes, and vegetables. Poultry, goats, and milk are also produced on the island.

Although sugar sales are no longer what they used to be, the sugar industry is still Jamaica's largest employer. Sugarcane is also used in the manufacture of another famous Jamaican export—rum.

Although it is illegal, marijuana (called "ganja" by many islanders) is a popular crop in Jamaica. Jamaican marijuana is smuggled into the United States and many other countries throughout the world. The drug is also widely used within Jamaica. The United States government has worked hand

Wood carvings for sale at the Harbour Street market at Montego Bay. Tourism contributes an estimated $2.5 billion a year to Jamaica's economy.

in hand with the Jamaican government to try to stop the production and distribution of Jamaican marijuana.

Living Below the Poverty Line

Jamaicans are among the poorest people in the Caribbean. Teachers in Jamaica make the equivalent of about U.S. $3,000 a year. That is almost one-tenth the salary most beginning American teachers make. Unskilled laborers are paid anywhere from U.S. $18 to $30 a week, or just slightly more than $1,500 a year. Many of Jamaica's unskilled laborers work in the sugar industry. In 2002 the World Bank listed Jamaica as 93rd in the world in a ranking of countries by per capita income. One-third of the Jamaican population lives below the official poverty line.

(Opposite) A Jamaican man prepares a goat for cooking during Cudjoe Day celebrations. Cudjoe was a Maroon leader who fought the British in the 18th century. Since gaining independence, Jamaica has maintained a strong relationship with Great Britain. (Right) Queen Elizabeth II attends a reception in Kingston during her official three-day visit in February 2002.

4 "Out of Many, One People"

THE MOTTO OF Jamaica is, "Out of Many, One People." This is because the island's nearly 2.7 million people come from many diverse ethnic backgrounds, yet all consider themselves to be Jamaican.

The Many

For much of Jamaica's history, blacks were slaves or manual laborers. Jamaicans were used to making assumptions about each other based upon the lightness or darkness of a person's skin. The lighter a person's skin color was, the higher social class that person might obtain.

Today, thanks to the black nationalism movement led by Marcus Garvey in the early 20th century, black Jamaicans have a newfound sense of pride and identity. However, some Jamaicans still make class distinctions based upon skin color. Whites, who are a minority, most often occupy the top of the economic and class structure. This has created resentment among many of Jamaica's darker-skinned citizens, both wealthy and poor.

Whites constitute a very small minority in Jamaica—just 0.2 percent. Yet many are among the island's wealthiest citizens. Some of Jamaica's whites are poor, though. Many are of Scottish, Irish, Welsh, or German descent. Many of them also have black blood in their family, although they rarely admit it. White Jamaicans are usually European immigrants or their descendants.

East Indians are another important ethnic group in Jamaica. Many Hindus traveled from northern India to Jamaica during the days following the abolition of slavery. They worked as cheap laborers or as indentured servants on plantations. After earning their freedom or saving enough money, many Hindus moved to Kingston and prospered as independent merchants. The East Indians also introduced ganja to the island of Jamaica.

Members of the Jamaican bobsled team compete in the 2002 Winter Olympics in Salt Lake City, Utah.

Quick Facts: The People of Jamaica

Population: 2,680,029 (July 2002 est.)
Ethnic groups: black, 90.9%; East Indian, 1.3%; white, 0.2%; Chinese, 0.2%; mixed, 7.3%; other, 0.1%
Age structure:
  0–14 years: 29.1%
  15–64 years: 64.1%
  65 years and over: 6.8%
Population growth rate: 0.56%
Birth rate: 17.74 births/1,000 population
Death rate: 5.45 deaths/1,000 population
Infant mortality rate: 13.71 deaths/1,000 live births

Life expectancy at birth:
  total population: 75.64 years
  male: 73.65 years
  female: 77.73 years
Total fertility rate: 2.05 children born/woman
Religions: Protestant, 61.3%; Roman Catholic, 4%; other, including some spiritual cults, 34.7%
Languages: English, patois English
Literacy rate (age 15 and over who can read and write): 85% (1995 est.)

All figures are 2002 estimates unless otherwise indicated. Source: CIA World Factbook 2002.

Jamaica is also home to approximately 5,000 Chinese. They, too, came first as indentured servants and cheap laborers. Like the East Indian Hindus, many Chinese became independent businessmen. During the 1970s the Chinese population decreased dramatically, as many Chinese left Jamaica for the United States and Canada. This mass exodus was a direct result of the political and drug-related violence that erupted throughout Jamaica.

The Maroons are one of Jamaica's oldest ethnic groups. They are the descendants of former slaves who ran away from the Spanish and British. The Maroons lived in their own communities and waged *guerrilla* warfare against the colonists to avoid recapture. Today there are Maroon settlements in Charlestown, Accompong, Moore Town, and St. Mary's. The highly independent Maroons primarily govern themselves from within. They retain some self-rule, existing almost as separate states within the nation. The Maroons have kept alive many old African customs that date back to the days of their ancestors across the sea.

Two of Jamaica's smallest ethnic groups are the Jews and the Lebanese. Many of the original Jews who arrived in Jamaica were fleeing from religious persecution. The Lebanese came to Jamaica and began selling cloth and clothing. Both groups have become very successful in their own ways. The Jewish population of Jamaica has been quite prominent in politics. The Lebanese population has become a dominant force in the world of business.

The Language

The official language of Jamaica is English. The most commonly spoken language of Jamaica is a Jamaican *patois*, sometimes referred to as Creole. Patois (pronounced PA-twah) is a kind of variation on a standard language. Jamaican patois is a mixture of English, Portuguese, African, Rastafarian slang, and Spanish.

Although it has roots in the English language, most English speakers from outside Jamaica would be hard-pressed to understand Jamaican patois without studying it first. For example, a "labba mout'" is someone who talks too much. "Schoolers" refers to students. A "rude boy" is an outlaw or a criminal. The term for a rowdy person is "leggo beast." The term used to refer to God is "Jah."

Greetings are a bit easier to understand. The most common greetings using Jamaican patois are "Everyt'ing irie?" and "Everyt'ing cool, mon?" The first is asking if everything is all right. The second asks if everything is cool. *Mon* is often used to address both men and women, although it is the word for man. *Woman* is generally pronounced without the "w" and becomes "oomon."

The Jamaican language is full of fanciful sayings. Many of these sayings have logical meanings behind them, however. If you hear, "All fruits ripe," you are being told that everything is fine. If someone says, "Dem jus begin fi dead," he or she means, "they almost dropped dead," or that they were surprised or amazed.

Education

Education in Jamaica is mandatory until the age of 15. Unfortunately, many rural students do not attend school that long, despite the law requiring it. When students do complete primary school, they must then take a competitive placement exam to see if they will be accepted into a secondary school. Those who complete secondary school must then take competitive exams to try to gain entrance into the nation's universities or vocational schools. In Jamaica, there are more students than there are seats available in the secondary, vocational, and university classrooms.

The public education system in Jamaica is much poorer than the typical school system in the United States. Very few Jamaican public schools are wealthy enough to afford computers. In rural areas, the schools are lucky to have electricity and running water. A teacher shortage throughout Jamaica, caused by low wages and poor working conditions, has raised the student/

Jamaican musicians greet tourists arriving on cruise ships, Montego Bay.

teacher ratio tremendously.

Jamaica's private schools are a different matter, however. Parochial (religious) schools in Jamaica are among the best in the nation. The problem for most Jamaican children, however, is that the cost of a private education is well beyond the limited incomes of their families.

Arts, Music, and Culture

African culture is still an important part of Jamaica. Folktales about Anansi the spider, a legendary African hero and trickster, are the favorite stories of many Jamaican children. These moral teaching tales are based on earlier stories passed down through the oral traditions brought over from Africa.

Dance and theater are a large part of Jamaican culture. The city of Kingston is the island's center for the arts. Here visitors and residents alike flock to see African, contemporary, and classical dance troupes. Jamaican

The most famous reggae performer is Bob Marley (1945–1981). In the late 1970s Marley and his band, the Wailers, brought this Jamaican musical form to international attention with such hit albums as *Natty Dread* (1974), *Exodus* (1977), and *Uprising* (1980). Bob Marley's music remains very popular today.

dance troupes are often involved in theater productions, as well.

Theater productions in Jamaica are generally performed using the patois language. The plays that seem to be most popular in Jamaica often deal with the plight of the poor, the struggles of women to achieve equality, or the turbulence and trials of Jamaica's history.

The most famous of all Jamaican theater productions is the annual National Pantomime. The National Pantomime was initiated in 1941. Although "pantomime" means gestures without words, the National Pantomime is far from a silent production. It often lampoons, or makes fun of, political and historical figures and events. It also often uses such beloved Jamaican characters as Anansi and his friend Tacooma, who dance, sing, and spin wonderful Jamaican folktales for their audience. This yearly musical comedy is performed in Kingston's Ward Theatre.

Music is an important part of Jamaican life. Bob Marley, the famous reggae singer and songwriter, is a national hero. Although best known for reggae, Jamaica is home to many musicians who play American jazz or Caribbean music like calypso and *soca*. There are also quite a few military marching bands in Jamaica.

Music is played seemingly everywhere in Jamaica. Outdoors, it is hard not to hear some type of song. Buses traveling the busy streets of Kingston, storefront loudspeakers, beach party disc jockeys, and outdoor cafés all merrily spill music into the humid island air. Even Jamaican dance halls are often simply mobile sound systems set up in outdoor locations. They are run by DJs who play Caribbean rap songs.

Rastafarians

Rastafarians are a group of Jamaicans who practice the religion of Rastafarianism. This Christianity-based philosophy holds that blacks are one of the 12 lost tribes of Israel. Rastafarians also believe that the spiritual home of the black race is Ethiopia in Africa. Jamaica is home to more than 100,000 Rastafarians.

Rastafarians are known for wearing a special hairstyle called *dreadlocks*. On the island, people often refer to this hairstyle as "dreds." Not all Rastafarians wear dreds, however.

Bob Marley is Jamaica's most famous Rastafarian. He wore dreds and sang songs of both religious and political significance. His backup band was called the Wailers. He became well known in Europe and the United States, where reggae music remains popular.

(Opposite) The largest city in Jamaica is Kingston, the capital, with a population of about 650,000. (Right) An aerial view of Port Antonio. The capital of Portland Parish is quiet but has a beautiful harbor and homes and churches that date back to the early 19th century. Fort George, which looks over the harbor, was built in 1729.

5 Parishes and Cities

JAMAICA IS BROKEN UP into 14 political zones referred to as parishes. These are Clarendon, Hanover, Kingston, Manchester, Portland, St. Andrew, St. Ann, St. Catherine, St. Elizabeth, St. James, St. Mary, St. Thomas, Trelawny, and Westmoreland. After parishes, the nation is divided into cities.

The three largest cities in Jamaica are Kingston, with a population of approximately 650,000; Spanish Town, with a population of nearly 100,000; and Portmore, with a population of nearly 98,000. The next three largest cities are Montego Bay, Maypen, and Mandeville.

Kingston

Kingston is the largest city in Jamaica as well as the nation's capital. Over one-third of the population of Jamaica lives in and around the city of

Tourists sunbathe on Mo Bay, Jamaica, as a small plane flies overhead.

Kingston. Kingston sits between two contrasting natural landmarks, the Blue Mountains and the Caribbean Sea. The city is a study in economic opposites, with small shanties sitting alongside modern high-rises. Street vendors with pushcarts, motorists, and goats share the streets of this city. Shopping plazas dwarf poor street hustlers peddling their wares.

Although poverty is a problem in Kingston, there are many things to do and see in the city. Visitors flock to the Bob Marley Museum. This museum is dedicated to the life and music of the late Jamaican reggae master, Bob Marley, who died in 1981. The National Gallery can be found on Ocean Avenue. Here Jamaican art from the 1920s through the present day can be viewed and enjoyed.

Not everything to see in Kingston is indoors. In the northern part of the city, William Grant Park is surrounded by streets that Jamaicans refer to as the Parade. In the center of this park, which was once home to an old fortress, sits a quirky wedding-cake-shaped fountain.

Kingston's harbor is the seventh-largest natural harbor in the world. Along its wooden wharfs, brown pelicans rest as fishermen tie their boats to the docks.

Spanish Town

Spanish Town is another interesting city in Jamaica. Spanish Town, once the capital of Jamaica, is now Jamaica's second-largest city. It is located in St. Catherine Parish, a mere 14 miles (23 km) away from Kingston.

Spanish Town was established in 1534 as St. Jago de la Vega and is said to be one of the oldest continuously occupied cities in the Western Hemisphere. In the past, the city's residents became known for their dedication to a statue of Admiral Lord Rodney. The admiral

A farmer digs up yams near Accompong, St. Elizabeth Parish.

saved Jamaica from invasion by the Spanish and French in 1782. When the capital of Jamaica was transferred to Kingston, Spanish Town's statue of Admiral Lord Rodney was moved to the new capital. An angry group of Spanish Town residents followed the statue to Kingston. In their attempt to kidnap the statue and return it to Spanish Town, the statue lost one of its hands. To appease the angry residents, authorities eventually returned the

Laundry hangs outside of shacks in a shantytown in Montego Bay, one of the largest cities in Jamaica. Although Montego Bay is Jamaica's most popular tourist destination, few visitors are allowed to see this aspect of life on the island. Unfortunately, many Jamaicans live below the poverty line, and unemployment and crime are high in slums like this one.

statue to Spanish Town and placed it once again in its city square.

Spanish Town is also home to a church that sits on one of the oldest foundations in all of Jamaica. The Cathedral of St. James was originally a Catholic Church built in 1525. Once known as the Catholic Chapel of the Red Cross, the structure was rebuilt in 1908.

Another historic site is Spanish Town's bridge over the Rio Cobre. This bridge is a Jamaican national monument. It is said to be one of the oldest cast-iron bridges in the Caribbean.

Portmore

Portmore, a suburb of Kingston, is also located in St. Catherine Parish. Most of its residents are middle-income Jamaicans who commute to Kingston every day for work. Much of the city of Portmore has been built upon filled-in wetlands that lie to the west of Kingston.

Portmore is known for its shopping centers and fast-food restaurants. It is a relatively modern city. In many ways, today's city of Portmore is the result of the efforts of Jamaica's Urban Development Corporation. It was expanded and developed by the Urban Development Corporation to provide a home for Kingston's middle-class workers.

Portmore may be modern in many ways, but it still dances to the same musical beat as the rest of Jamaica. The Portmore Festival Village is a large entertainment complex on the north side of the city. Called JamWorld, this complex has been the host site for the Reggae Sunsplash, an annual international reggae music festival. It hosts many reggae concerts throughout the year, and Jamaicans often gather there to enjoy music and companionship.

Montego Bay

Montego Bay, which has a population of about 90,000, is located on the northwestern coast of Jamaica. The city is Jamaica's most popular tourist destination. The area was first settled by the Spanish in 1510. They called it "Bahía de Mantega," which means Bay of Lard. This unpleasant name came from the Spanish colonists' main export: lard made from wild pigs.

Today, Montego Bay is the capital of St. James Parish and one of Jamaica's largest cities. Tourist resorts line its beaches, where visitors from around the world flock to enjoy swimming, boating, diving, and fishing, among other water activities. The surrounding countryside is home to several historic plantations. Croydon in the Mountains, a plantation 20 miles (32 km) inland from Montego Bay, was the birthplace of one of Jamaica's national heroes, Sam Sharpe.

Montego Bay is currently the host city for the annual Reggae Sumfest, an international reggae music festival. It also boasts a wide variety of shopping, from upscale stores near the resorts to several busy, outdoor craft markets showcasing local goods.

Maypen and Mandeville

Maypen (or May Pen), a city of about 50,000, is located in south-central Jamaica near the Minho River. The city is home to the famous Royal Jamaica cigar factory.

To the northwest of Maypen, nestled in the Manchester Mountains at an elevation of more than 2,000 feet (610 meters), is the city of Mandeville, whose population is about 40,000. Sometimes called "Little England," Mandeville boasts a Georgian-style courthouse, a village green, country churches, and simple cottages that recall an English village. During the colonial period, many plantation owners summered in Mandeville because of its pleasant climate. Today the city remains a destination for vacationers.

A Calendar of Jamaican Festivals

January

New Year's Day is celebrated on January 1.

The Accompong Maroon Festival, January 6, dates back to the 19th century and features traditional dancing, feasts, and ceremonies.

February

Bob Marley Day, February 6, honors the famous musician.

Ash Wednesday is a Roman Catholic holiday, the date of which varies from year to year.

March

Commonwealth Day is celebrated on the second Monday in March.

April

During Carnival, costumed groups parade and dance in the streets of many Jamaican cities. Two Roman Catholic holidays that are celebrated on different dates each year are Good Friday and Easter Sunday.

June

During this month the Ocho Rios Jazz Festival is scheduled. This annual jazz festival features numerous jazz concerts in several cities.

July

Reggae Sumfest, in Montego Bay, is an annual music festival that showcases local and international reggae musicians.

August

Emancipation Day is celebrated on August 1. This day commemorates the day in 1838 when all of Jamaica's black slaves were freed. Celebrations begin the evening before and continue until dawn.

On August 6, Jamaicans observe Independence Day. This holiday celebrates the date on which the British granted independence to Jamaica. It is marked by numerous cultural celebrations, including art exhibits, dancing, theater, and parades.

October

National Heroes' Day is celebrated on the third Monday in October. This holiday is held in honor of Jamaica's "right excellent" national heroes, including Paul Bogle, George William Gordon, Marcus Garvey, Nanny of the Maroons, Alexander Bustamante, Norman Manley, and Sam Sharpe.

December

Jamaicans celebrate Christmas on December 25.

The next day, December 26, is Boxing Day, which is based on an English holiday. Jamaicans give small gifts to service workers such as postmen and newspaper deliverymen and celebrate the Christmas season at community fairs and dances.

A Calendar of Jamaican Festivals

Jamaica's rich heritage is reflected in the nation's holidays and festivals.

Recipes

Banana Fritters

3 bananas
6 tbsp flour
1 1/2 tsp baking powder
2 tbsp sugar
1/2 tbsp grated nutmeg
1/3 cup milk
Oil

Directions:

1. Crush bananas till they are creamed.
2. Combine flour, baking powder, sugar, and nutmeg.
3. Add milk and bananas, then mix.
4. Pour oil into a frying pan.
5. Use an oiled spoon to scoop batter into frying pan.
6. Deep-fry in pan till brown and crisp on the edges.
7. Drain on paper towel and serve.

Curry Chicken

1–2 lbs skinless, boneless chicken
Lemon or lime juice
2 tbsp curry powder
Dash each of onion, thyme, garlic, pepper
Salt to taste
3 tbsp oil

Directions:

1. Cut chicken into small pieces, then rinse with lime or lemon juice. Drain chicken.
2. Sprinkle chicken with curry, onion, thyme, garlic, pepper, and salt, and let season for awhile.
3. Pour oil into skillet and heat.
4. Add chicken and cook until done.
5. Serve over white rice.

Banana Porridge

3 green bananas
1/2 cup flour
1/2 tsp salt
5 cups water
1 cup milk
Sugar to taste
Nutmeg
Vanilla

Directions:

1. Peel and grate bananas.
2. Add flour and salt to grated bananas and mix well.
3. Beat mixture with fork while adding small amounts of water until smooth.
4. Boil remaining water in a pan.
5. Pour mixture into boiling water, stirring constantly to prevent lumping. Stir until mixture thickens.
6. Continue cooking, add milk, and let mixture simmer over low heat.
7. Cook for about 30 minutes.
8. Add sugar, nutmeg, and vanilla to taste.

Beef Soup

2 qt water
1 lb soup bones or stew meat
1/2 lb carrots, cubed
1/4 lb turnips, cubed
1 lb pumpkin, cut up
1/2 lb chocho (small, green, pear-shaped squash),
    cut up
1 lb yellow yam, cut up
1 sprig thyme
2 stalks scallion
1 tbsp salt

Directions:

1. Boil soup bones/stew meat in water.
2. Cut up vegetables, yam, and chocho and add
   with seasonings to soup.
3. Bring to a boil.
4. Simmer uncovered until yam is cooked all the
   way through.

Vegetable Callaloo

1 lb callaloo (leafy, spinach-like vegetable similar
    to turnip or collard greens)
1 medium onion, chopped
1 tbsp margarine
1/4 cup water
1 scotch bonnet pepper (very hot pepper, ranging
    from yellow to red in color)
Black pepper
Salt to taste

Directions:

1. Wash callaloo leaves.
2. Cut up callaloo leaves.
3. Sauté onion in margarine.
4. Add cut-up callaloo leaves and water and stir.
5. Cover saucepan and cook callaloo until tender.
6. Add whole scotch bonnet pepper.
7. Sprinkle with pepper and salt.
8. Simmer, then serve.

Glossary

abolition—the elimination of slavery.

alumina—a mineral composed partly of aluminum, found by itself or in bauxite.

bauxite—a mineral used to manufacture aluminum.

cay—a small island made of coral.

Communist—someone who believes that the state should own all property and that goods and services should be divided equally among all workers.

dreadlocks—a hairstyle formed by matting or braiding locks of hair.

enfranchised—given the right to vote.

Greater Antilles—an island chain that includes Cuba, Hispaniola, Jamaica, and Puerto Rico.

gross domestic product—a measure of the total value of goods and services produced in a year.

guerrilla—a private citizen who wages war against the government, usually as part of a small, quickly moving group.

indentured servant—a person who agrees (by contract) to work for a specified length of time for a particular employer, usually in exchange for travel expenses, food, and shelter.

limestone—a type of soft, chalky rock.

martial law—a period, usually during an emergency, when the government puts the army in charge of law enforcement.

mulatto—an individual who is of mixed black and white ancestry.

parish—a political subdivision of a country, often corresponding with an original religious community.

Glossary

patois—a variation on a standard language that is often spoken regionally, that may include special vocabulary and pronunciations, and that often combines elements from several languages.

plateau—a flat area of land at high elevation.

socialist—characteristic of policies that favor extensive government involvement in business and in the distribution of goods and services to citizens.

universal suffrage—the right to vote for all adult citizens.

Project and Report Ideas

"Right Excellent" Research Report

Write a report on one of the following "right excellent" heroes of Jamaica:

Paul Bogle   Sir Alexander Bustamante
Marcus Mosiah Garvey   George William Gordon
Norman Washington Manley   Nanny of the Maroons
Sam Sharpe

Be sure to explain why the subject of your report is considered to be a "right excellent" hero in Jamaica!

"Top Ten" Time Line

Create an illustrated time line of Jamaica's history to hang in your classroom. It should display what you believe are the top 10 most important dates in Jamaican history. Be ready to defend your choice of dates to your classmates and teacher.

Music Reports

Write a report about one of these types of Jamaican and Caribbean music:

- calypso
- reggae
- soca
- limbo

Find out how that type of music started, who its important performers have been, and whether the music has a specific type of dancing associated with it. Play some recordings of the music for your class when you present your report.

Project and Report Ideas

Jamaican Artists

Colin F.

1. Research the life and art of this famous contemporary Jamaican artist. Explain what his impact has been on the visual arts in Jamaica.
2. Try to create some art that represents your vision of Jamaica based on Colin F.'s unique style.

You can find several examples of Colin F.'s work here: **http://www.colin-f.com/gallery1.html**

Mallica (Kapo) Reynolds

1. Research the life of the artist Mallica (Kapo) Reynolds. Explain how she influenced visual arts in Jamaica.
2. Study examples of art created by Mallica Reynolds. Create your own artwork based upon her style, techniques, and media (the type of art she liked to do).

You can find an example of her work here: **http://www.unt.edu/bryantart/html/k48.htm**

Edna Manley

1. Find several examples of the sculptural work of Edna Manley. Create your own sculpture based on her artistic techniques and style.
2. Explain how Edna Manley helped to change the visual arts in Jamaica. What was one of her biggest achievements?

You can find an example of Edna Manley's work here: **http://www.iadb.org/exr/cultural/jamaica/photo2.htm**

Chronology

Ca. A.D. 700   Arawaks settle in Jamaica.

1494   Columbus arrives.

1509   Juan de Esquivel settles Jamaica, calling it Santiago, as Columbus had.

1509–1655   Spanish occupation of Jamaica.

1655   British capture Jamaica.

1670   Treaty of Madrid officially turns Jamaica over to British.

1655–1838   Slave economy develops, based on agriculture and large plantations.

1808   Abolition of slave trade.

1831   Christmas Day Rebellion.

1838   Slaves emancipated.

1838–1938   Peasant economy develops, based on small farms.

1840   Assembly adopts law enabling majority of blacks and those of mixed race to vote.

1865   Morant Bay Rebellion.

1944   All Jamaican adults gain right to vote.

1962   Jamaica becomes an independent country.

1968   Jamaica helps found CARIFTA (Caribbean Free Trade Area).

1972   Michael Manley elected prime minister.

1980   Violence rocks Jamaica during election campaign.

1988	Hurricane Gilbert wreaks havoc across the island.
1992	Michael Manley resigns as prime minister due to health reasons; his deputy, Percival J. Patterson, is sworn in as prime minister.
1993	P. J. Patterson is elected to a term as prime minister by a wide margin.
1997	The People's National Party consolidates its political power by winning 50 of 60 seats in the national assembly.
2002	P. J. Patterson wins reelection as prime minister, becoming the first Jamaican prime minister to win three consecutive terms.

Further Reading/Internet Resources

Baker, Christopher P. *Jamaica*. Oakland: Lonely Planet Publications, 2000.

Barlas, Robert. *Jamaica*. Milwaukee: Gareth Stevens, 1998.

Gottlieb, Karla Lewis. *The Mother of Us All: A History of Queen Nanny, Leader of the Windward Jamaican Maroons*. Lawrenceville, N.J.: Africa World Press, 2000.

Luntta, Karl. *Jamaica Handbook*. Emeryville, Calif.: Avalon Travel Publishing, 2000.

Manley, Michael. *Up the Down Escalator: Development and the International Economy: A Jamaican Case Study*. Washington, D.C.: Howard University Press, 1987.

Sherlock, Philip, and Barbara Preston. *Jamaica, the Fairest Isle*. London: Macmillan Education Ltd., 1992.

Watson, G. Llewelleyn. *Jamaican Sayings: With Notes on Folklore, Aesthetics, and Social Control*. Gainesville, Fla.: University Press of Florida, 1991.

Winter, Sylvia. *Jamaica's National Heroes*. Kingston, Jamaica: National Press Commission, 1971.

Travel Information

http://www.jamaicatravel.com
http://www.discoverjamaica.com
http://travel.state.gov/jamaica.html

History and Geography

http://www.odci.gov/cia/publications/factbook/

Economic and Political Information

http://www.cabinet.gov.jm/
http://www.mct.gov.jm
http://www.jamaicaelections.com

Culture and Festivals

http://www.moec.gov.jm/
http://www.nlj.org.jm/

Jamaica Tourist Board
64 Knutsford Boulevard
P.O. Box 360
Kingston 5, Jamaica, West Indies
1-800-233-4JTB

Jamaican Embassy in the United States
1520 New Hampshire Ave., NW
Washington, DC 20036

United States Embassy in Jamaica
Jamaica Mutual Life Centre
2 Oxford Rd., 3rd Floor
Kingston 5, Jamaica

United States Consulate in Montego Bay
St. James Place, 2nd floor
Gloucester Ave.
Montego Bay, Jamaica

Index

Contributors

Senior Consulting Editor **James D. Henderson** is professor of international studies at Coastal Carolina University. He is the author of *Conservative Thought in Twentieth Century Latin America: The Ideals of Laureano Gómez* (1988; Spanish edition *Las ideas de Laureano Gómez* published in 1985); *When Colombia Bled: A History of the Violence in Tolima* (1985; Spanish edition *Cuando Colombia se desangró, una historia de la Violencia en metrópoli y provincia*, 1984); and coauthor of *A Reference Guide to Latin American History* (2000) and *Ten Notable Women of Latin America* (1978).

Mr. Henderson earned a bachelor's degree in history from Centenary College of Louisiana, and a master's degree in history from the University of Arizona. He then spent three years in the Peace Corps, serving in Colombia, before earning his doctorate in Latin American history in 1972 at Texas Christian University.

Colleen Madonna Flood Williams is the author of over 10 nonfiction children's books. Colleen resides in Homer, Alaska, with her husband Paul, son Dillon Meehan, and their dog Kosmos Kramer.